ANGELS BY MY SIDE

Jeff Breddy

The characters and events portrayed in this book are fictitious. Any similarity to real persons, living or dead, is coincidental and not intended by the author.

Cover design by: Art Painter
Library of Congress Control Number: 2018675309
Printed in the United States of America

ANGELS BY MY SIDE

This collection of poems all have a spiritually inspired theme and have been written by me over the last five years.

I would like to share them with you in the hopes that not only will you enjoy them as standalone poems but that they will provide a source of contemplation.

DESTINY

Upon a weathered bench I sit
Wrapped up warm against winter chill
Minutes pass by unnoticed
For my gaze is fixed on the scene below
Crashing waves give birth to foaming plumes.

Sighing I rise for it's time to leave
But what is that emerging from the surf?
Entranced I watch the transformation
From watery spray to rearing horse
Its' cold grey eyes chill me to the core.

A connection has been made
Like long lost friends we watch each other
As we close the gap between us
With just a moment's hesitation
I climb upon the horses back.

My ears are filled with wondrous noises
From whispering bubbles to thunderous roars
Then I hear them, those long forgotten voices
As my steed carries me to God knows where
Their words of wisdom give me courage.

THE INTRUDER

Step after reluctant step, I climb the well-worn stairs
Fingers trace the balustrade, then a stack of tired old chairs
My wavering torch illuminates, dust motes taking flight
Across my face a chill wind blows, and then I'm filled with fright
For once dead speakers come to life, and music crackles out

With all my senses overwhelmed, statue-like I stand
The music I now recognise, as being Glen Miller's band
With courage gone I turn to flee, and come face to face
With a group of laughing soldiers, running at great pace
All but one sweep past me, disappearing with a shout

Blue eyes a twinkling, he murmurs, I'm very glad you've come
His stone cold lips take my breath away, leaving me quite numb
Confidently his hands explore my body, fearsome and so bold
I feel his sense of urgency, and willingly surrender to his hold
Have I gone and lost my mind? What's this all about?

The speakers falter, the music dies and he begins to waver
Speaking with great urgency, he wants to ask of me a favour
But then he's gone, the spell is broken, down those stairs I leap
I'm running 'till I'm out those doors, then collapsing in a heap
Only then do I spot, the crumbling cinema's sign, KEEP OUT.

CHERRY BLOSSOM

Blush tinged petals rain down on me
Early morning sun glints on dewy grass
Bare footed I feel the chill, but I don't mind
My fingers caress the rough old bark
And I smile to myself as I remember

So long ago, and yet, as if yesterday
When we were young and newly wed
Beneath this tree we sat and spoke
Of dreams and goals that lay ahead
And I smile to myself as I remember

Kneeling down beside you, my favourite
I showed you life's tiny wonders
Your face lit up as a bug took flight
Then frowned as I winced in pain
And I smile to myself as I remember

Cherry blossom, like life is fleeting
Here today but gone tomorrow
But do not cry for the fallen petals
For soon there will be fruit
And I smile to myself as I remember

A QUIET PLACE

Will you now enter, your quiet place
She says with a smile, upon her face
From around the room, come gentle sighs
Taking a deep breath, I close my eyes
And try to still, my questioning mind

So many thoughts, buzz around my head
Silence I seek, but get noise instead
One by one, I bat each thought away
They can be dealt with, another day
With mind now blank, what is there to find?

Use your mind's eye, comes a whispered thought
Creating a link, I've just been taught
Insights I've gained, like how to receive
Memory links, to help them believe
That it’s love that forms, the ties that bind

The divine spark burns, within us all
Driven by love, I have heard their call
That quiet place, a thing to treasure
Power of thought, is without measure
Part of the whole, but one of a kind

THE GIFT

Waves of perception, roll invisibly
Sensing the unseen, still hidden from me
Figures coalescing, before my eyes
Four guides smile knowingly, at my surprise.

Pearls of unspoken wisdom, fill my mind
As gentle loving arms, around me wind
Slowly at first, they begin their dancing
Increasing tempo, becomes entrancing.

No longer four, now a glittering one
A hand reaches out, their task almost done
Mine touches theirs, we are one and the same
Tears well inside, yet I'm glad that they came.

Then they are gone, leaving a gift behind
Placed in my hands, it will serve to remind
That when I need help, they'll always be there
Together we journey, lessons we share.

A TALE OF TWO STUDENTS

Step by step, I explore, the flame lit corridor
Flaking painted walls, foot-worn tiles, adorn the floor
Crumbling symbols, my fingers trace, their ancient grain
Half-forgotten memories, racing through my brain
If only I could understand, what they are telling me.

I shake my head, and step, into a darkened room
Freezing for a moment, there's someone in the gloom
From the shadows, out he steps, grinning bold as brass
Posing there, dressed in black, he will not let me pass
He says, he's come to join me, on my quest you see.

Accustomed to the light, I cannot help but laugh
For to the right, I spy, a softly glowing bath
Kneeling down, he dips his hands, throwing me a smile
His meaning's clear, my clothes, become a carefree pile
Now immersed, with eyes closed, my cares are floating free.

A gentle splash, startles me, from my floating rest
He's baptised himself, water's running off his chest
I'm chuckling now, at the absurdity
Of this play-full, revealing, serendipity
I wonder, what's the lesson, spiritually?

The scene it fades, yet there we remain, side by side
Mirrors appear, reflecting aspects, we can't hide
From devilishly dark, to pure, angelic white
An old man's voice, quietly crackles, with delight
We are complete, our master's here, two becomes three.

Words of profound wisdom and love, he shares with us
Then it's time to go, they've become, nebulous
Alone in the corridor, I start to reflect
'Bout life and death, both, deserving of our respect
Tell them I'm here, and ok, had been his parting plea.

ANGELS

Silt laden waters, turgidly flow
Over pastures flooded, long ago
A figure hides, where the rushes grow
Feeling his way, stumbling and slow.

He'd tried to escape, didn't belong
They'd hunted him down, and did him wrong
Shackled in chains, by the vanished throng
For fear they might hear, his siren song.

He fell to his knees, tired and broken
Silent prayers, he left unspoken
But they were more, than just a token
His pleas were heard, angels had woken

As yet unseen, the angels took flight
Asleep then, he didn't see their light
As they freed him, and wept at the sight
Of this fallen angel's sorry plight.

Loving arms, carried him tenderly
Loving thoughts, helped him sleep peacefully
Loving hearts, offered sanctuary
Is this fallen angel, you or me?

TOUCHING LOVE

Shelter from the summer rain, we seek
A well placed shop, to our rescue comes
Among shelves full of tat, we take a peek
Bargain hunting, while doing our sums
Hidden treasures, we are sure to find.

There it is, a snowy marble heart
Half-forgotten, looking rather sad
Now placed in my palm, I give a start
Visions I see, am I going mad?
A bright room with white nets, comes to mind.

Shaking my head, I'm looking again
I'm back in that room, but not alone
Gazing outside, she's hiding her pain
Longing to hear, the ring of the phone
Why have they gone? She's always been kind.

A lump in my throat, I glance around
Has anybody noticed, my little trance?
I'll keep that heart, it's only a pound
I pray that one day, I'll get the chance
To open their eyes, them that are blind.

A NEW LIFE

Go on, they said, it will be fun
Be quick, they said, it's just begun

Be brave, they said, have no fear
Worry not, they said, we'll be here

By your side, they said, you cannot fail
I reply, with, a baby's wail

MEMORIES

Memories come, memories go
Each day's the same, passing so slow
To many, I'm just an old hag
Yet my spirits, refuse to flag
Even though, some might wish, they did.

As a young maid, off to the hills
With my beau, I sought teenage thrills
Such joyful times, but soon found out
My father gave, the lad a clout
From then on, my lovers I hid.

Cut glass crystal, refracting light
Scintillating, diamond bright
Bringing it slowly, to my lips
Taking dainty, hesitant sips
Of the heady, amber liquid.

Closing my eyes, against the sun
Releasing my hair, from the bun
Inhaling deep, crisp autumn air
I can be free, without a care
Men broke my heart, so I got rid.

Have I regrets? Maybe a few
No more questions, I beg of you
Leave me alone, please let me be
I'm enjoying, that memory
Play nicely, or farewell I'll bid.

THE NEED FOR SPEED

Summer sun, beating down on me
Tarmac road, stretching hazily
Into silent, dusty distance
I ride without a backwards glance

Once more, I feel the need for speed
Faster faster, those voices plead
My metal steed, joyfully roars
I laugh out loud, my spirit soars

Bikes you see, is what I'm about
Until one day, my luck ran out
Stopped in my tracks, so to say
Now other games, I have to play

I shake my head at the vision
And recall that it's my mission
To pass on his message of love
And guiding thoughts sent from above

THE GARDENER

Order he seeks, in a garden overgrown
With mission accomplished, many seeds he sows
But his work was in vain, for in they have flown
Each seedling was eaten, by raucous black crows

Yelling at the birds, he chases them away
A chorus of squawking, loud flapping of wings
Drained he sinks to his knees, and begins to pray
Oh why can't he get right, the simplest of things?

No answer he hears, for his mind is racing
With dark vengeful thought, as he sits on his feet
The rough paving cracks, his fingers are tracing
Yet smiles knowing that, nature is hard to beat

Standing once more, his expression turns rueful
Surveying the wreckage, of that last battle
Time spent in the garden, is always joyful
But now he needs, to return to his castle

As he's turning the handle, of the back door
He senses the approach, of those seldom seen
Their unspoken thoughts, he is hearing once more
Once inside the kitchen, to sit down he's keen

He closes his eyes, knowing they'll shed tears
Feelings of love, wash through his mind and his soul
Sage words of advice, calmly ring in his ears
To love all God's creations, should be his goal.

THE READING

Churning thoughts I can sense
Glancing up, I catch your eye
Why the frown? Why so intense?
Yet you join me, with a sigh
Smiles exchanged, we now commence.

Brain engaged, no time to waste
My kaleidoscopic cards
Are slowly, thoughtfully placed
Each they speak, like well-versed bards
Their wisdom, I have embraced.

Word by word, pictures I paint
Intuitively spoken
All in truth, no lie will taint
Of a heart, that was broken
But was borne, without complaint.

Tears well up, ready to spill
I feel loved ones, drawing near
Guidance, they try to instil
Living your life, without fear
Taking their love, if you will.

A DRYADS TALE

I must face the truth, the season's slowly changing
Nothing stays the same you see, no use denying
I can feel it in my bones, creeping up on me
Cold damp mornings, pale sun hangs, over misty lea.

A slow tide of orange, comes flowing down the hill
Loud colourful prequel, to silent winter chill
I hold on hard, but still, I feel them slip away
By the score they're falling, with each windswept day.

To you it may sound wrong, I'm giving up the fight
A peaceful release, for me you see now feels right
I blissfully sleep, beneath softly falling rain
Black silhouetted branches, are all that remain.

Then freezing nights, with the moon and stars, shining bright
Petrifying the ground, with its grip icy tight
But winter will pass, and a new cycle begin
In spring I shall wake, as the sap rises within.

So I say to you, as you walk by unaware
You must learn to let go, live your life without care
Life's nothing but a cycle, for me and for you
So salute the past, but please, welcome in the new.

A PLACE CALLED HOME

One quick prayer
Then a leap of faith
No going back
Energies I feel
Are building within.

I still my mind
And slowly breathe in
Thoughts flashing by
So fleeting and fast
I sense them all.

Now taking shape
I see her clearly
Stood beside me
Messages of love
Silently said.

Memories shared
I relay them all
Feelings of peace
Washing over me
Then tears we share.

A vision I'm shown
Flashes of colours
Beings of light
Wonderously bright
A place called home.

REUNION

Haloed monolith, stark against the skies
A welcome sight, true beauty in my eyes
Time worn runes, almost gone without a trace
Rain soaked moss, greenly cloaks its stony base.

I've been searching, for oh so many years
But now I'm here, I find I'm close to tears
Through time and space, now back to where I left
When stones shone new, and my lover bereft.

I stop awhile, then ponder what to do
Sitting amongst, flowers of every hue
Glancing up, I watch birds flying overhead
Then at the path, aeons old with smooth tread.

Silently killing, mists shrouding the sun
Feeling no fear, I know it has begun
A shape's coalescing, no longer hiding
Towards my flung open arms, she's gliding.

ELECTRIC BLUE

A message sent as if by chance
With a casual fleeting glance
From her to me a lightning bolt
Transfixed thoughts judder to a halt

Those eyes once a chocolate hue
Are now a bright electric blue
Oh so slowly it dawns on me
The meaning of what I can see

Fleshy matrix had once concealed
A hidden truth to me revealed
Through a spiritual vision
As part of my guided mission

A simple truth it proves to be
That spark of life which glows in me
Links me with all humanity
And makes my life reality.

SAILING

Her graceful arching lines smoothly slice
Through each and every turquoise wave
Gulls crying out their lofty advice
While sails flap and catch the wind they crave

Statue-like he stands braced before me
Weathered features creased up in a smile
Piercing eyes scan both the sky and sea
Then meets and holds my gaze for a while

Together we sail through day and night
Little is spoken but much is thought
About dark times and those filled with light
Of chances given and lessons taught

What can I say to my guiding star?
How do I repay what's without price?
Freely given as we journey far
A Heartfelt 'Thanks' he says will suffice.

HOME AT LAST

In circular silent contemplation we sit
Each staring intently at the central focus
Expectations rising as the power's building
A virtual campfire in a safe space clearing
Spiritual flames flickering warming my soul

A spinning shimmering vortex of energy
Whirling faster and stronger giving protection
Figures coalescing they're plain to be seen
Now standing beside us we're feeling them too
They guide and support us when we need it the most

My attention is drawn to a lady in blue
Her habit is flaring as she dances with mirth
Briefly she stops and with a thoughtful expression
Toasts our good health while holding a glass of Blue Nun
Then leaves with a smile saying "You're home at last".

SAILING

Her graceful arching lines smoothly slice
Through each and every turquoise wave
Gulls crying out their lofty advice
While sails flap and catch the wind they crave

Statue-like he stands braced before me
Weathered features creased up in a smile
Piercing eyes scan both the sky and sea
Then meets and holds my gaze for a while

Together we sail through day and night
Little is spoken but much is thought
About dark times and those filled with light
Of chances given and lessons taught

What can I say to my guiding star?
How do I repay what's without price?
Freely given as we journey far
A Heartfelt 'Thanks' he says will suffice.

THE TREE OF LIFE

Furrowed bark spirals above expansive roots
Branches overarching providing leafy shade
Child-like I gaze in awe at this mighty tree
I soak in every detail then reach up
To touch its scintillating emerald leaves

A connection's been made I feel the life force
That craggy wood is transmuting into bronze
I watch in wonder as bronze now becomes gold
My fingers trace the ever changing ridges
Revealing the once hidden angelic light

That majestic tree's now a whirling column
Of love and energy drawing me closer
Like a moth to a flame that cannot hurt me
No longer alone for there's others nearby
They have heard the calling to come home again

I sense shadowy figures gliding past me
Once lost and confused they're regaining themselves
Truly spirited folk on a journey bound
Entering the light without a backward glance
Gladly returning to the place they came from

The power is fading my attention returns
To the room full of people so unaware
Of the glorious visions that I've just seen
While my love's soothing tones were filling the air
Taking them travelling while safe in their chair.

A GIFT & A CURSE

By giving heartfelt messages of love
We seek to ease pain and help heal the sick
Connecting with those in heaven above
A priceless special gift being psychic

We do it for Spirit and those hurting
Yet some accuse us of playing a trick
Of mystical powers we're exerting
Both a gift and a curse being psychic

To withstand the world we need to be strong
A mindful turn of phrase and skin that's thick
Discerning truth from lies and right from wrong
Sometimes it feels a curse being psychic

So I say to those who don't understand
And ignorantly dismiss us so quick
If only I could share visions unplanned
You'd see the true gift of being psychic.

ALL HAIL HALLOWEEN

Fast approaches the autumn equinox
And folk are busy turning back their clocks
Excited kids can both be heard and seen
They know that soon it will be Halloween

To each door they run and then loudly knock
Trick or treat they shout knowing they will shock
Expectant faces painted gorily
All dressed to impress horrifically

How ironic this childhood innocence
Celebrating the dark's omnipotence
The gap between two worlds will soon be closed
'Tween good and evil day and night opposed

Time is nigh the sun has finally set
Mists rise up coating all with dewy sweat
Portals open the hunting has begun
A black web of psychic threads have been spun

With kids in bed it's time to walk the dog
A lonely place your stroll becomes a jog
Dancing shadows are filling you with dread
Too late! They're here and messing with your head

Despairing voices whisper in your mind
Your feet take flight too scared to look behind
Home once more against the door you lean
Until you hear her ask "Where have you been?"

HALL OF LEARNING

My vision clears I'm stunned by the view
Above me a sky of icy blue
Below bright eddies of energy
In front a white marble effigy

At least twice my height and polished bright
Each carved detail glimmers in the light
In his hands he holds an open book
Head bent yet at me he seems to look

I'm sure I heard a soft stony sigh
A little unnerved I walk on by
Following the path I'm meant to tread
That leads me to the building ahead

Pantheon-like it impresses me
When seeking knowledge it's where to be
The Hall of Learning stores the records
Of our karmic paybacks and rewards

I knock on the door and step inside
Waiting for me is my spirit guide
Smiling he asks what I hope to learn
I reply that for truth I do yearn

To a question I've asked by the score
How many lives have I lived before?
The answer which I often debate
Chuckling he nods then asks me to wait

He returns with a dusty volume
It will take time to read and consume
Sitting down I flick the book's pages
Each one details lives through the ages

How can there be so many of me?
Suddenly the truth is clear to see

I'm part of the great divinity
And will be for all eternity

THE CHOSEN ONE

At the beginning starting from scratch
Life seems simple no whiff of a catch

Running carefree truly a child's game
Unaware that fate is taking aim

Crossroads encountered choices to make
Mind all awhirl which path shall we take?

Heart and mind loudly battle it out
Trying to find what life is about

Views ever changing never the same
Mistakes will be made who takes the blame?

Our feet took those steps led by our head
But what if our heart had led instead?

Steep rocky trails cause hurt for the soul
But they bring us closer to our goal

Pain brings clarity aids decisions
Baggage released with swift excisions

Taking time out we rest for a while
Enjoying the view each heady mile

Stretching out before us river like
Adventures await! Let's start that hike

Our routes may differ this time around
By searching within clues can be found

Of other paths and of times gone by
When love and lives we shared you and I

Such a winding path, this chosen one
Only completed, when life is done

A WHITER SHADE OF RAINBOW

Purple morphing, into blue
Becoming green, right on cue
Yellow now, no, wait orange
Then it's red, again all change

Pick a colour, I am told
Full of joy, I'm feeling bold
Then I pause, how do I choose
From these, scintillating hues?

Ha! My brain is full of tricks
Just one? Let's give them a mix
Beating arms, I'm taking flight
Colours merging, into white

On I go, now flying high
I hear laughing, then a sigh
For an angel, watches me
Waiting oh, so patiently

He frowns, yet his eyes they smile
This lesson's, taken me a while
For thinking, outside the box
Will help me, survive life's knocks

THE GUIDING LIGHT

Tiredness overcomes me
The evening's getting late
My fire's reduced to ruby embers
Nestling in the grate

With eyes slowly drooping
I sink further into my chair
Enveloped in slumber's peace
I do not have a care

I'm woken with a jolt
Angelic light dispels the gloom
Smiling calmly, radiantly
His presence fills the room

Wide awake and overjoyed
For my guide is here once more
Strewn across the table now
Are plans over which we pore

I get confused, how do I choose
The route that's right for me?
Doesn't matter which, he says
There's lessons in each you see

THE BOOK OF MAGIC

Into the magician's room you creep
Softly tiptoeing while he's asleep
Gentle snoring is filling the air
Hugging his pillow without a care

Around the room you silently tread
Your nerve's hanging by a single thread
At last you find what you've been looking for
A leather bound book sat on the floor

With a deep breath you carry the book
To the window for a better look
Excited now you walk to the door
With the prized piece of magical lore

A quiet escape you have in mind
But the door is now locked you will find
Sat on his bed he watches you squirm
Laughing calls you a thieving book worm

Then gestures you're to sit by his side
The truth he wishes you to confide
There's price to be paid nothing's for free
A wily old man that mage you see

Still clutching the book you count to ten
Before speaking you count ten again
You're seeking within the spells you need
To the problems you wish to be freed

Nodding his head he gives permission
For you continue with your mission
With trembling hands you open it wide
The surprise you feel is hard to hide

Each page is blank there's nothing to see
The wise old mage smiles and nods sagely

The truth is simple now here's the clue
All the solutions lie within you.

SEEKING INSPIRATION

Last night I asked for a word you see
To help ignite the poet in me
Straight back it came its vision I heard
Ah perfect I thought that's just the word

My brain's engaging while thoughts take flight
Loudly squawking their poetic insight
But it's time for sleep my thoughts must slow
Not quite yet for my guide's made a show

Here's another word for you says he
With just a touch of sweet irony
Now acceptance must also be used
No chance I grumble your task's refused

But by the morning my mind has changed
And my poetic thoughts been rearranged
For into this poem two words can go
And still keep up the spiritual flow

That guide knows better and is so wise
Vision uses more than just your eyes
While acceptance is not giving in
Together they bring your truth within.

SHARING

I'm all of me and then some more
Take my hand so we can explore
A world that most have never seen
By their choice or 'cos I'm not keen
To share with those who just don't care

So now we're here what can you see?
Waves and bands of pure energy
Our thoughts and actions intertwine
Before long our love will combine
I share with you my soul laid bare

I see myself in some of you
But not just me the whole world too
Animals or plants all the same
Connected by life's sparkling flame
We share our lives so please beware

What has been will happen again
Unless we can somehow refrain
Love and respect should be our game
Better than seeking those to blame
I'll share my all if you'll be there.

THE GAMES WE PLAY

You need to choose is it black or white?
Killing the king's the aim of the fight
But what if you saw just shades of grey?
The thrill of winning might fade away

Not your thing? How about rolling some dice?
But Lady Luck doesn't always play nice
Just when you think you maybe winning
She'll change her mind and send you spinning

How about playing another game?
So pick some cards no two are the same
You'll obey the rules? Or will you cheat?
But no way will you admit defeat

Who you're beating and the games you play
Are all up to you it's just your way
Tell me though is your conscience quite clear?
Better make sure for the end game's near.

CUP OF TEA

Can you spare me a minute or two?
I have a secret to share with you
Before I do I'd like a favour
A cup of tea that I can savour

That's right my dear just a cup of tea
If that's not too much to buy for me
Just one sugar and a dash of milk
You're such a sweetie with hair like silk

Go on then I'll have a biscuit too
Am I hungry? Sadly yes that's true
Oh never mind this isn't about me
More about you now I've drunk my tea

Swilling the dregs and reading the leaves
Sat before me is someone who grieves
Tears have fallen yet your smile is bright
As blue as your eyes so locked up tight

Don't get upset please give me your hand
I will take a peek at all that's planned
Your life's mapped out by so many lines
Advice I'll give by reading the signs

Believe me or not it's up to you
Love it or leave it which will you do?
I can't change it that's your fate you see
Thank you though for that nice cup of tea.

LITTLE SHOP OF DELIGHTS

Welcome to our little shop of delights
Claims the banner aglow with angelic lights
So come on folks will you please step inside
The doorman invites his arms open wide

You're curious now so what's there to see?
Over the threshold you step carefully
For the lighting is dim but just enough
To see shelves lined with all manner of stuff

It stocks everything for all your needs
For the road ahead wherever it leads
With a personal guide stood by each shelf
They're ready to help you choose for yourself

It's a funny old place this little shop
Very untidy and could do with a mop
A quick lick of paint would do it no harm
But that I guess is all part of its charm

How do I know all this I hear you ask?
I'm a member of staff set with the task
Of providing you with a few insights
About our little old shop of delights.

HOLD MY HAND

A steely angel stands silently
Yet his message I hear quite clearly
A battle's coming it's been planned
Please give me strength take hold of my hand

High on a hill above rolling mist
He's gesturing with his other fist
Parting the fog revealing the land
Without once letting go of my hand

A subtle motion catches my eye
My name's being called a silent sigh
I feel you close together we stand
Your loving presence touches my hand

What's was hidden would cause me alarm
Now it's in sight I know there's no harm
I know what to do I can withstand
Still it'd be nice if you'd hold my hand

And stay with me for a little while
Your happy thoughts are making me smile
But our link is now just a tired strand
All alone no one's holding my hand.

RUBY TUESDAY

In a sea of tears
Sitting three rows back
Faces lighting up
Thanks to a wise-crack

I'm learning loads
About a life unknown
Bittersweet images
To me are shown

Stood by the bier
So still and serene
She's solid to me
To others unseen

Now closing my eyes
For pain I'm feeling
It's hitting like waves
Leaving me reeling

Released from her chains
And the earth she's free
A link has been made
I know she sees me

Silent tears flowing
Mine dotting the floor
But they're tears of joy
She's suffering no more

While we say goodbye
To Ruby Tuesday
She's giving them hugs
And her love three-way

The music has stopped
As we interweave

One last hug from us
Then it's time to leave.

ACROSS THE DIVIDE

You've been gone for nearly thirty years
Gently passing through our veil of tears
I remember well your love for me
Like a mother you will always be

Beneath life's bridge swirling water's flowed
Many long years have served to erode
All my sharp edges are worn down smooth
And what used to cut now serves to soothe

These times are strange I'm no longer sure
What I have seen and had to endure
Leaves me quite numb and feeling alone
I wish I could call you on the phone

I am sure you heard my thoughts today
Just for a moment with me you'll stay
My hairs stand up our energies merge
An invisible psychic static surge

I feel your love no words are spoken
There is no need our link's unbroken
To and fro our many thoughts flow free
Her mission complete I'm now esprit

MY GUARDIAN ANGELS

Iridescent feathers filling my mind
Arms supporting me our thoughts entwined
My guardian angels are with me once more
Each one protecting a guiding mentor

Their heavenly laughter's filling my ears
Love and devotion allaying my fears
Opening my eyes I see the same view
That my mind's senses had sworn to be true

Three angels surround me wings open wide
Electric blue eyes glimmering with pride
Billowing robes of white silver and gold
Bright blinding auras a sight to behold

Holding my arm Azriel throws me a smile
And casually says I've known you a while
For the Angel of Death helps souls depart
While I help those that have a grieving heart

Umbriel joins us he's the Angel of Fate
Deceptively kind he will dictate
The path I'm travelling along in life
And ignoring his will causes more strife

Fiercely kind Ariel is wafting her wings
Bringing joy to my soul until it sings
It's down to her that I have green fingers
And in my garden her perfume lingers

But time is passing I must let them go
I'm truly grateful for the love they show
Now they've gone a question I want to ask
Known me for a while? Is life just a masque?

THE HAND THAT GUIDES

How to describe something without shape?
My mind's clattering like ticker tape
Long thought chains forming a tangled mess
Clarity sought instead I digress

How do I sense what cannot be seen?
Not with my eyes but what's in between
Focused within I sense the without
Energy's flowing I have no doubt

How do I know what it wants from me?
A whispered reply comes silently
If you've lost your way we're here to guide
And if confused we'll help you decide

But how do I know what to believe?
Is this a trick that's meant to deceive?
Energy's swirling all around me
Filling my heart and soul completely

Bursting with love I cannot deny
All that I have seen with my third eye
I've been touching the divine I'd say
When holding the hand that guides my way

TOUCHING MEMORIES

In old Church Street there's a little shop
A treasure trove where I love to stop
Objects old and new sit side by side
All are sparkling and polished with pride

Standing within an Aladdin's cave
Senses hit by a historic wave
Lost amongst more garish merchandise
Shyly hiding from my roving eyes

The dark contrast has attracted me
As has the smooth rich mahogany
The antique dealer catches on quick
He clearly never misses a trick

From the shelf he carefully retrieves
The wooden candlestick he believes
Is Georgian or Victorian may be
Holding it close a vision I see

Sunlight streams in I'm feeling its heat
While sat relaxing feeling replete
Ladies voices laughter and chatter
Cups of tea and cakes on a platter

A charming scene from so long ago
When life was precious and time ran slow
This candlestick I so want to buy
But can't afford it the price too high

Reluctantly I surrender it
Once more to the shelf where it will sit
Waiting to share precious memories
Across the divide of centuries

ANGELS WATCHING OVER ME

Downy feathers brushing tenderly
Through my soul with divine energy
For when I'm in need they're heaven sent
Healing love their angelic intent

I can't believe I'm that deserving
Of their devotion so unswerving
From the beginning they've been with me
Offering their help invisibly

Protecting my life I swear it's true
When accidents come out of the blue
And crossroads I meet choices to make
Helping me discern the true from fake

Their presence I love as they love mine
Kindred spirits part of the divine
Soul brothers and sisters we are one
Joined by a thread like fine silver spun

We take it turns to come down to earth
Experiencing life for all it's worth
Those left behind will watch through the veils
Wings at the ready like feathered white sails

TOUCHING BASE

The eye of my mind opens once more
Sensing a room with studious décor
So warm and safe with its fiery glow
Outdoors the night is pure indigo

Lost in thought I don't hear him approach
My guide my mentor my lifetime coach
Behind his desk he's once more sitting
Enrobed in brown that's quite befitting

He throws me a smile then holds my hand
The heartaches I've hidden now expand
Through my defences he sees each one
Gently he takes them until there's none

My heartaches are thrown into the fire
This sacred yet emotional pyre
It's time to reflect upon my fate
Oh Jesus I sigh he'll now berate

Catching that thought he's laughing at me
Then shaking his head I'm fine you see
I'm tying up those loose ends I'd left
Painful it may be but I'm quite deft

Correcting mistakes long overdue
Learning missed lessons more than a few
So no more tears I have to believe
I'm still on track with more to achieve

AMBER & GOLD

Deep in the woods it silently weeps
From a wound a gold tear slowly seeps
That forest and tree have long since gone
But the memory of them lives on

A beautiful gem cupped in my hand
Protected within a golden band
Both to be treasured for what they are
I keep them safe too valuable by far

But how do you know if they're genuine?
Study them closely and peer within
Just like us if they seem too perfect
Then they are most probably suspect

For amber can be cloudy or clear
But much like plastic it can appear
So look for faults and natural flaws
If there are none this should give you pause

And all that glitters may not be gold
The rich and the fools don't feel the hold
That yellow metal has over them
To a hollow life it will condemn

Real or fake? How much does it matter?
How strong is your faith? Will it shatter?
If what you perceive proves to be real
That to me is their golden appeal.

THE TRAVELLER

Feeling drowsy I lay down next to you
Your relaxed smiling face filling my view
Together we drift but so far apart
You into slumber me a journey's start

A raging father with millennia span
That central creator worshipped by man
Life giving destroyer holds all in thrall
An enormous shining nuclear fire ball

Mercury runs quickly a wayward child
Too close to the parent its face defiled
In the heat of the day iron flows free
But come night fall it freezes instantly

Sister Venus you have surprised us all
Losing your water was life's curtain call
Barren lands hidden beneath clouded veils
Of acid raindrops and all that entails

Oh dear mother Earth how I love you so
The vibrancy of life's making you glow
Teeming turquoise oceans and clouds pure white
And backlit by your moon's reflective light

Mars was the Roman god of war I'm told
If that's so he's fighting a war grown cold
A little brother too small to fight on
And now the atmosphere is all but gone

Glittering moonlets and rocks are tumbling
Spatial disorder colliding rumbling
They'll never unite always careering
Because big brother is interfering

Banded Jupiter he wants to be king
But grew too slow now forever throwing

His roiling weight around and holding court
With his moon wives a true royal consort

Then on to Saturn he's holding court too
Rhea Tethys Titan to name just a few
Handsome and bold his rings seen from afar
He's tilting and spinning like a film star

Uranus you've been the butt of every joke
Remaining serene with that pale green cloak
The victim of a planetary crash
Ninety degree tilt result of that smash
Turbulent Neptune last of the giants
The first to be found using man's science
Thanks to its ices a beautiful blue
Ammonia and methane give it this hue

Sun rise on Pluto is a dim affair
Too distant you see for there to be glare
Together with Charon forever more
Eternal winter with no chance to thaw

So cold it's almost absolute zero
Travelling light I'm my super hero
Change of focus and I'm back in my bed
But those astral sights remain in my head.

SPIRIT'S CUP

Laying in bed weary and broken
I'm screaming words left unspoken
Tired of life and all that entails
Wind battered yacht with tatty sails

Up to the eyeballs with this stuff
No more spirit I've had enough
And with that thought I fell asleep
Slumbers benefits I shall reap

A new day and what did I find?
Two messages left to remind
Spirit had listened to my cries
Coincidence to my surprise

First a like the next a request
Both have left me feeling so blessed
To have been touched and lifted up
Quenching my thirst from Spirits cup

THE SCRYING GAME

So young one
You want to see ahead
And seek guidance
On this path you tread

Unburden what's been
Troubling your mind
And with my help
Your truth we will find

My crystal ball
It patiently waits
Your thoughts are stilled
A link it creates

Between me and you
The here and now
Future glimpses
That Spirit allow

So many options
Lay before you
With each new thought
There's another view

Choose well young one
Or you'll be to blame
Your truth's revealed
In the scrying game

WORDS

Words are always running through my head
I hear them clearly though seldom said
Been strung together like pearls entwined
Simple meanings become redefined

Inspiration I'm often given
Without warning and feeling driven
Through sight and sound I will make it clear
Imparting meaning to words I hear

With my words a sculptor I've become
Shaping your thoughts while vocal chords strum
Rising and falling moods and words flow
Until you're lost in my poetic show

Visions you've seen and emotions felt
Led by the ear poetically svelte
For I wanted you to see those words
Invading my head like raucous birds

A RAINBOW IN MY HEAD

Autumnal mists swirling in my head
Creeping shadows filling me with dread
Needing to flee but where can I go?
Time is fleeting and nothing to show

Now dawn is here with sun glowing red
Anger's raging with a fiery tread
Searing its way through my muddled brain
All that remains is a crimson stain

Red fades to orange before too long
Creative energies flowing so strong
The joy of living filling my soul
Sharing of pleasure's become my goal

The sun has risen golden yellow
Thoughts of myself I'm chilled and mellow
No longer caught by dark self doubting
Self confidence grows like shoots sprouting

Emerald leaves like fluttering kites
Their healing colours my heart excites
High over head and all around me
Each precious leaf waving lovingly

Trees left behind I look to the sky
Of its blue beauty I want to cry
A lump in my throat I need to clear
My voice will be heard and without fear

The sky's now a dark indigo blue
And strewn with stars a true astral view
My eyes may be closed but still I see
All that glows with truth spiritually

Feeling the chill I wrap my cloak tight
Imperial purple fitting just right

The hood on my head worn like a crown
A king of knowing and great renown

But what is this if it's not the end?
These colours are beginning to blend
Into a pure brilliant gleaming white
I am now one with Spirit's pure light

BELIEVE

Woken abruptly
From a dreamless sleep
I'm out of my bed
And downstairs I creep

Voices and music
Are calling to me
Drawing me closer
Hypnotically

Spices and perfumes
Filling my senses
Welcoming smiles
Overcome my defences

Bright coloured silks
And sheets of white cotton
All remind me
Of treasures ill-gotten

Weaving my way
Through crowds I continue
I spy an old crone
All bone and sinew

Crooking a finger
She's grinning at me
Patting the ground
I sit obediently

In her rheumy old eyes
I sense her pain
Yet her wisdom she wishes
Me to gain

Holding my hand
I hear her silent thoughts

Then I'm feeling
A tugging of my shorts

Her other hand
Has slipped a note inside
It's a secret
She wishes to confide

Then she's gone
And I know it's time to leave
Back at home
The note simply says "believe"

MESSENGER

Come here my love won't you take my hand
There's so much for you to understand
Through this messenger my voice you'll hear
So please don't shake there's nothing to fear

He does his best to connect with me
But he's only human don't you see?
In your eyes he's rather stern and cold
He's just protecting his heart of gold

Now where was I dear? Oh yes that's right
I'm here for you in your darkest night
When all your troubles seem to overwhelm
Like demons from some unearthly realm

You're sensing the truth is being spoke
And your heart's healing no longer broke
So come closer please and feel my love
Sent to you now from heaven above

ANGELS BY MY SIDE

When storm clouds gather as they often will
Others may panic I choose to stand still
It's not I don't care or like to be wet
But weather to me is simply no threat

I'll tell you a secret that's plain to see
But please just keep it between you and me
You see I have an angel by my side
No wait a minute don't scoff or deride

Hold on don't leave there's no need to be mad
I'm not having you on please just be glad
When I'm in need to my side they will fly
And my flowing tears they always wipe dry

I see in your eyes you still don't believe
Thinking that fact and fiction interweave
I have never said these angels have wings
Like you and me they're just human beings

But how special these people are to me
Each has been caring as caring can be
Lifting me up and then dusting me down
While helping me lose my permanent frown

I'm lucky you sec I have more than one
An army's helping get this battle won
For we are growing bolder with each stride
How can I lose with angels by my side

THANK YOU

How do I phrase what I want to say?
Expressing my thoughts could take all day
When travelling on life's hardest roads
Difficulties come in bucket loads

You'll never know the impact you made
To my flagging soul you gave first aid
Lifting me up and dusting me off
Rousing my brain with a gentle cough

Please don't be shy you know who you are
Because you see there's a shining star
That can't be hid as much as you try
A flame that burns in both you and I

You saw in me a little of you
Seen by many understood by few
A link was made and so it began
Those spirited ones had hatched their plan

Whether near or far it doesn't matter
The fear filled vision you helped shatter
Giving me the strength to continue
Now with all my heart I say thank you

DARK TEMPTATIONS

Rain is pummelling the window pane
Each watery punch soaking my brain
Stirring the maelstrom that is today
A mask I wear to hide my dismay

Loud is the tempest roaring within
Pain creating emotional din
Distracting me from external life
Yet mirrors my worry and our strife

But what is that I can see inside
A room of dark things trying to hide
No need to conceal they're part of me
Not always nice nor always pretty

Ah I see I've your attention now
Your interest is piqued but anyhow
I'm too focused on my storage room
To care if you judge me or presume

My dark temptations are calling clear
Their whispering tones loud in my ear
Try Medusa's rage and baleful gaze
Speak with furies calamitous phrase

Or will it be the tearing apart
Of a soul losing its pain filled heart
Try swimming across a whirling pool
Not letting go that blazing jewel

It's plain to see you don't understand
Dismiss this with a wave of your hand
I've told you the truth simple and plain
Dark temptations can only bring pain

With a sigh I refocus my mind
Loosening the knots and rope that bind

My thoughts are free to resume their flight
Towards a higher goal and shine bright

THE NOMADIC HERMIT

Nomad or hermit call me what you will
For try as I might I just can't keep still
My feet and brain are always on the move
Ever seeking novel ways to improve

To stop and stare is a momentary thrill
While catching my breath before that next hill
I study the paths that lay before me
From top of the mount beneath windswept tree

Decisions decisions which should I choose?
My attentions caught I start to peruse
A narrow track almost hidden from view
Excitement is rising for this one's new

Give me a moment I wish to reflect
For the hermit within needs to connect
Me to the knowledge and skills I will need
If this new adventure is to succeed

Memories gathered and put to one side
Like buried treasure inside I will hide
Until they are exchanged along the way
With those true seekers not wanting to play

So I'll stay for a while hanging around
I'm taking it all in both sight and sound
The hermit you see is searching for more
While the nomad's walking on as before.

A WHITER SHADE OF FLIGHT

Whirling and swooping in clouds of white
Flocks of random thoughts are taking flight
Discordant lines in pure harmony
Laughter bubbling at the irony

I feel love and light supporting me
Enrobing my soul completely
Floating free I can go where I please
Powered by joy I'm moving with ease

Remembering that when a young child
I had dreams of wings and flying wild
Soaring and swooping above the ground
But on landing they couldn't be found

If only I'd known they're always there
I'd have flown to heaven without care
To thank the angel who gave me wings
So I could fly and see wondrous things

Believe me or not the truth's out there
You'll have to look and perhaps to care
The mind and body aren't the same things
All you will need is a prayer and wings

LIFE

What is it life that you want from me?
Silence is all I'm getting you see
Oh come on now please give me a clue
I'll keep it just between me and you

Yes I'm looking but I still can't see
What do you mean there's a trail for me?
I think you're now just playing a game
Where is this trail? And what is its aim?

Ah I think I've found one of your hints
For ahead of me are faint footprints
Curious now I decide to follow
Those steps into a leafy hollow

Then out again into blaring sun
I'm wondering what have I begun
Yet still these steps keep leading me on
It's getting dark the sun's almost gone

What now life? Why have you led me here?
Is this a test or something to fear?
Have I gone too far and lost my way?
I need your help do I have to pray?

Thank God at last I can hear your voice
What do you mean that it was my choice?
You're telling me those footprints weren't clues?
Just some walker enjoying the views

Hey! Okay! I will calm myself down
I'm cross with myself feeling a clown
How can I trust what is told to me?
I see you're nodding that means you agree?

From now on it's my instincts I use
To avoid mistakes and others ruse

Ah now you're grinning your secret's out
The penny's dropped that's what life's about.

THE LIGHTHOUSE

At the point where land joins raging sea
Stands the lighthouse tall as tall can be
Built by man to save all passing ships
From the rocks and deadly tidal rips

Curving smoothly upwards to the sky
White painted walls designed to defy
Those angry destructive crashing waves
Seeking prey for their watery graves

Night time comes the bright lanterns are lit
With mirrors in place the beams transmit
Across the ocean for all to see
A true beacon of hope and safety

Morning's here but no sign of the sun
Fog rolling in its game's just begun
The lighthouse siren begins its wail
An eerie sound like a love sick whale

Be as that may the keeper keeps on
Until all danger has been and gone
That man is brave you have to agree
By doing that job when most would flee

A good friend said that light house is me
Standing so firm while feeling lonely
Defying the tides of life to heed
Those that are in spiritual need

UNIVERSAL GUIDE

For far too long I'd been feeling down
My smile being replaced with a frown
But my mojo's back without a doubt
I know I've regained my psychic clout

What had dried up is now flowing free
Hearing all those connecting with me
Change is coming the picture's shifting
Once again my vibration's lifting

To follow the herd I had no need
Trust in myself to let Spirit lead
Quiet meditation's worked for me
I asked them what I needed to see

A vision began a gentle scene
Low rolling hills and a lake serene
Wooden bench beneath a Maple tree
And a figure sits waiting for me

Sitting beside him I say hello
He nods and smiles his face seems to glow
Without moving his face starts peeling
And a female face is revealing

Ever faster the peeling goes on
Until there are none they've been and gone
A perfect black void just a blank space
That should have been filled with my guide's face

But now I can see stars burning bright
Constellations of spiritual light
Ah now the meaning is clear to me
My guides and Spirit are one you see.

BREAKING LINKS

Lost within the morning fog
Just me and my little dog
How light and dark lines the street
This scene's eerily complete

I can sense you watching me
Shadowing invisibly
Your presence felt still unseen
Emptiness that's never been

Closer now I am quite sure
Your energy's far from pure
With my mind I'm scanning you
Seeking out each subtle clue

You're standing there clear as day
Dressed so smart with eyes of grey
Tell me now why are you here
And in my life interfere?

To keep me safe you reply
An angel a true good guy
Where are your wings? I retort
On display I would have thought

Hateful words you start to hurl
As they begin to unfurl
Demon black instead of white
Ha! I'm laughing I was right!

Time you went and left my sight
For I've called on Spirit's might
And wrapped you in purest pink
No more to me will you link.

THE TOTEM TREE

Deep in the woods stands the totem tree
Alone in silence where noise should be
Twisted and wounded by rusty nails
Covered in posters like tattered sails

Don't go near the warning signs declare
As if the tree was some monster's lair
Ready to grab any passerby
Ah but are the warnings truth or lie?

But how can it be the truth you see
And who nailed the posters to the tree?
I wonder sitting beneath its bows
I've drunk too much I begin to drowse

Dark fitful dreams are filling my mind
Lightning storms and writhing limbs entwined
Lashing rain mirrors rivers of pain
Freedom we want and freedom we'll gain

The dreams continue I've set it free
All nails removed I'm down on one knee
I'm pledging my love and feeling blessed
My beating heart is filling my chest

Then I'm awakened by a soft breeze
Being caressed by verdant leaves
And raised to my feet by snaking roots
Being brushed off by young silky shoots

I'm free to go yet here I'll remain
To help remove the old fear filled stain
That was nailed to my spiritual tree
For we're one and the same don't you see?

ME

There was a time when I hated me
So unaware of what I would be

A lonely feather caught on the breeze
Bourne aloft by a sense of unease

Needing to settle too scared to land
And torn in two with only a strand

Holding together this whirling mind
A slim silver strand that served to bind

There's more to me than I ever thought
Oh how well life's lessons have been taught

Before the mirror what do I see?
A man with a plan just to be me

Been around that block many a time
I'm feeling my age and past my prime

But truthfully with hand on my heart
Learning to love me was a good start.

LIGHT WORKERS

Light workers! Light workers! Hear my call
'Coz I have a message for you all
Shake off your doubts and what holds you back
And those dark whispers they're way off track

So ignite your golden light once more
Be that beacon like you were before
By guiding the way for those without
Your knowledge of spirit holds great clout

People and places can cause great pain
By chance or plan energy they'll drain
Dust off your shields and let that light out
Filling the void that's now all about

Light workers! Light workers! Hear my plea
Join me in Spirit's loving army
Shining the light on those that deride
And together we'll drive back the tide.

A GIFT FOR THE PRESENT

Headphones in place I'm ready to go
Closing my eyes with breath getting slow
Soft music plays his voice baritone
Urging me into that quiet zone

So relaxing I'm almost asleep
Then woken by a bird's startled cheap
In my mind I can see clearly now
That bird sitting on an old gnarled bow

Creaking gently in a summer breeze
In one of the many hedgerow trees
Blue sky above me green grass below
My hearts aflutter I'm all a-glow

Laying supine with head to one side
Showing the love that I cannot hide
Sitting cross legged he's dressed all in black
I now realise this was a flash back

To far off times and well before me
I was a maid with status lowly
My bosom is framed with tired old lace
Flushing with passion as is my face

There will be children of this I'm sure
I was young naïve and immature
Believing he'd be loyal and true
While facing his parent's angry spew

But that's yet to come and still unknown
And not why I'm here or to be shown
Live life fully enjoy each moment
And that is my gift for the present.

GUIDING ADVICE

Summer sun is setting in the west
Oh my days! I'm feeling truly blessed
The sky above fills with orange hues
But in the east it's a purple bruise

Through the meadow a path I'm making
Beneath my feet the ground is quaking
Against my legs grass blades are bending
While a harvest moon starts ascending

Ahead of me a tall stand of trees
Quiet voices carried on the breeze
Nearly there and a figure I spy
Before his hard stare I'm feeling shy

A Celtic warrior there is no doubt
Tattoos covering a body stout
Strong arms folded below spiked blonde hair
He's standing guard while casually bare

With a slight smile he lets me within
And now my adventure can begin
Into a fire lit grove I am shown
A druid upon a mossy throne

Sitting straight sporting a deer skull mask
He wants to know what I want to ask
So do I but that mask's been a shock
Off it comes clearing my mental block

The path I'm on is it right for me?
He replies you'll have to wait and see
Only when it's done will I realise
Just how much growth my soul will apprise.

ENERGY

A shining vortex energy shoal
Circles are whirling around my soul
Such fascinating incandescence
Can anyone else sense their presence?

Flickering ions both light and dark
Filling my vision leaving their mark
A double vision this earthly plane
Never the same will I be again

Believe it or not few seldom do
They are part of me like I am you
What feels solid is really porous
This energy surrounds and fills us

It's time to ride that tangible wave
And task my mind with a path to pave
Rocky or smooth? Which one should I choose?
Lessons to gain with nothing to lose

I run this race with clear certainty
Finishing will take eternity
And this learning journey's the real prize
It's how you can become knowledge-wise

So join me please on this roundabout
Whirling around why not scream and shout
Hold my hand 'coz you'll come to no harm
We can't be hurt that's energy's charm.

CHANGES ARE COMING

Changes are coming I've seen it so
Empty offices all in a row
Some will have reached the end of their life
Huge carcasses awaiting the knife

Those that are left will meet a new fate
Long gone are the days of working late
Slaves to the system have flown the coop
Planners caught in a perpetual loop

Homes for the young and homes for the old
We need homes if I may be so bold
So please less of the corporate greed
And more of meeting our basic need

For life love food and security
Time for man to show maturity
Take care of the whole not just the part
It may take some time but it's a start

Changes are coming you can be sure
For all of us whether rich or poor
Mother Nature's catching up with us
Our behaviour she wants to discuss

Why not give it some thought if you will
What are her truths she'll want to instil?
Count your blessings not what you have not
Changes are coming if you've forgot.

www.ingramcontent.com/pod-product-compliance
Lightning Source LLC
LaVergne TN
LVHW052054160826
845678LV00015B/3224